Farm Animals

Farming is the most important occupation in the world. Nearly all the food we
from crops and livestock raised on farms. In the past, many families barely raised enough food for themselves. The family raised cattle, chickens and hogs and grew crops and vegetables. Horses ploughed the fields. Since then, scientific advances have made farming increasingly specialised and productive. In some wealthy countries, each farmer produces enough food to feed up to 80 people. Farming has become an important business run by large corporations and is no longer a way of life as it was in the past. Today, smaller private farms provide food diversity and availability.

Across

3. This strong animal, once used to pull a plough, is now raised mainly for riding.
4. The female bovine is most often raised on a dairy farm.
5. Most of these animals are raised for meat on hog farms.
7. This animal has provided people with milk, meat and wool since prehistoric times.
9. A domestic one is raised for its meat and fur, for use in scientific research and as a pet.

Down

1. These are among the most important animals in the world because they provide both food and clothing.
2. Raising this animal for meat and eggs is a major industry.
6. This waterbird is raised for its meat and for its down (soft feathers).
8. We think of this animal as part of a traditional Christmas dinner.

chicken
cow
goat
goose
horse
pigs
rabbit
sheep
turkey

Homographs

Some words have more than one meaning. There are two clues for each word in the puzzle. Think of a word that fits both clues. Write the word in the puzzle.

Across

4. not heavy
   to set on fire
5. to conveniently arrange papers
   a tool with ridges used to smooth surfaces
7. an enclosure where stray animals are kept until redeemed
   to hit with a heavy blow
8. a big dance
   a round object used in sports

Down

1. a warning sound made by a kind of snake
   a baby's toy that makes noise when shaken
2. an herb, tree or shrub
   to put in the ground so that it will grow
3. friendly, generous
   sort or variety
6. part of the body at the end of the arm
   to pass or give something to someone
7. to have fun
   a story that is acted out on a stage

ball
file
hand
kind
light
plant
play
pound
rattle

Trucks

Trucks carry food to grocery stores, petrol to service stations, manufactured goods from factories to stores; nearly everything we eat, drink, wear and use has been delivered by truck. Trucks vary greatly in size. Most trucks have more powerful engines than cars and are built for rugged work. Manufacturers produce many different kinds of trucks. They are classified into three main groups: light, medium and heavy. The groups are based on gross vehicle weight, the combined weight of the truck and the load it carries.

Across

1. a popular, light-duty truck with an open bed
2. carries liquids such as milk, oil or petrol
4. a large, roomy, medium truck used for moving furniture or other bulky items
5. works at construction sites to unload material as the rear of the truck tilts the contents
7. mixes and pours a strong material that has many uses such as the foundation of buildings

Down

1. an all-purpose flatbed truck with rails, often used on farms
3. comes to our homes and businesses to collect refuse
6. a light truck popular with small businesses such as florists for delivering their goods

concrete
dump
garbage
van
pickup
platform
tank
panel van

Nursery Rhymes

Nursery rhymes have been passed on verbally for centuries. Every culture has its own nursery rhymes plus additional ones that have been adopted from other countries. There are many origins for the rhymes. Ballads, prayers, proverbs, tavern songs and fragments of ballads account for many of the rhymes. A nursery rhyme is a rhythmical poem that amuses or soothes young children. Many pass on cultural information and values and help children appreciate the sounds and rhythms of a language.

Cow
Humpty Dumpty
Jack
Jack and Jill
Little Bo Peep
London
Mary
Mouse
Old Woman
Peter
Spider
Three

Across

1. what ran up the clock
4. who went up the hill
6. who lived in a shoe
7. who was a pumpkin eater
8. what jumped over the moon
10. who lost her sheep
11. who had a little lamb

Down

2. what went up a water spout
3. who fell off a wall
4. who jumped over a candle stick
5. what bridge is falling down
9. how many men were in a tub

1.
2.
3.
4.
5.
6.
7.
8.
9.
10.
11.

Travel

Across

5. bring in case it rains
6. small note, usually with a photograph on one side, sent by mail
9. a day assigned by the government to honour a person, event or idea
10. a place to swim
11. a vehicle that travels on roads
12. a vehicle that travels in the sky
14. a person visiting a place from out of town
15. an object in which clothes and other items are packed

Down

1. a place for pets to stay while their owners are away
2. an object you buy to remember a place or time
3. a vehicle that travels over water
4. shows the location of roads, cities and landmarks
7. staying outdoors, even to sleep
8. a period of time where you don't attend school or go to work
13. a place that rents rooms to travellers
14. a vehicle that travels on rails

aeroplane
boat
camping
car
holiday
hotel
kennel
map
pool
postcard
souvenir
suitcase
tourist
train
umbrella
vacation

Spiders

Spiders are classified as arachnids. Unlike insects that have six legs, spiders have eight legs and have two main body parts, not three. Spiders have fangs and poison glands they use to capture animals, usually insects, for food. They live anywhere they can find food. There are 30,000 known kinds of spiders, but some scientists believe there are thousands more. Each species of spider has a different life span. Many kinds live for only a year. Wolf spiders live for several years. Some tarantulas have lived for 20 years in captivity. Spiders are helpful to people because they eat insects that destroy our crops and carry diseases.

bones
eight
food
insect
poison
silk
spinnerets
two
webs

Across

2. A spider's ________ make silk.
6. A spider's fangs hold ________.
8. A spider is an arachnid, not an ________.
9. A spider's body does not have ________.

Down

1. Webs are made of ________.
3. A spider has ________ legs.
4. There are ________ parts to a spider's body.
5. Spiders live anywhere they can find ________.
7. All spiders spin silk, but not all spiders make ________.

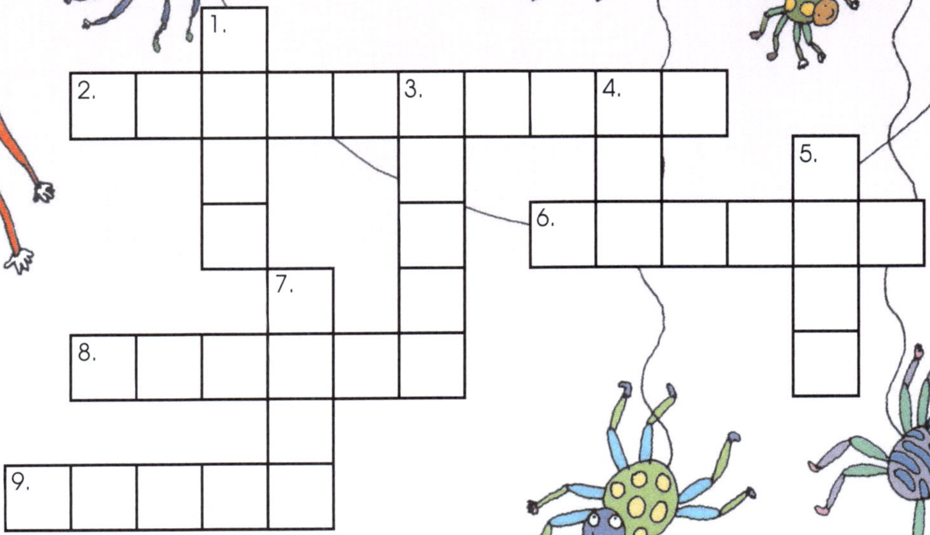

Insects

Insects are small six-legged animals. An insect's body has three main parts. Most adult insects have wings. They smell mainly with their antennae, and some taste with their feet. Many insects hear by means of their bodies. Others have ears on their legs. Although many insects do harm, they are an important part of the food chain. They are also an important part of our food production as they pollinate crops. Insects live almost everywhere on earth, although few insects are found in the oceans.

ant
bee
butterfly
dragonfly
firefly
horse fly
ladybug
mayfly
mosquito
termite

Across

1. queen rules
4. unsaddled
6. terminator
7. lacy, delicate wings
8. picnic pest
9. does not breath fire

Down

1. won't melt
2. vampire insect
3. pyromaniac
5. female bug

Word Sounds

What sounds do they make?

Use the clues to write the words in the puzzle.

Across

1.

3.

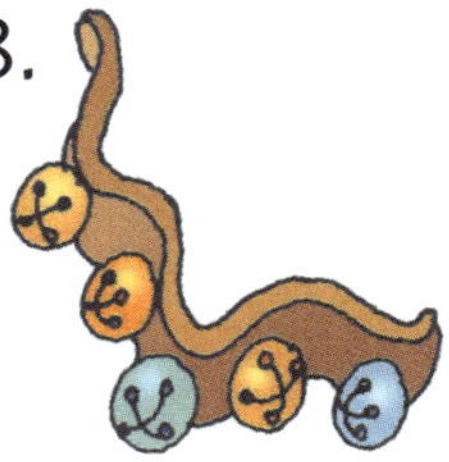

4.

6.

8.

Down

1.

2.

5.

6.

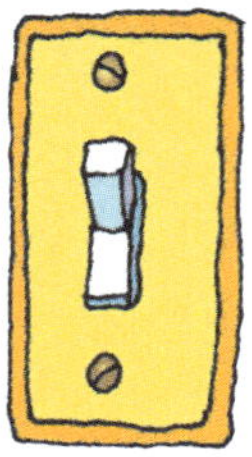

7.

Trees

Trees are the largest of all plants, some of which grow higher than three-story buildings. The giant sequoias of California are the oldest and largest living things. Trees continue to grow as long as they live and some trees live for thousands of years. A tree's leaves make food that helps the tree grow and keeps it alive. Many trees lose their leaves during winter, allowing the trees to rest. Other trees keep their leaves and stay green all year long. There are thousands of kinds of trees, some of which only grow in warm regions.

botanists
deciduous
evergreen
grow
food
roots
seed
soil
water
wood

Across

1. A tree has three main parts: (1) the trunk and branches; (2) the leaves; (3) the ________ .
3. One of the most valuable parts of a tree is ________ .
5. Most needleleaf trees are ________ .
7. The main job of leaves is to make ________ .
8. Scientists who study plants are called ________ .
9. Trees help conserve ________ and ________ .

Down

2. Most trees begin life as a ________ .
4. Most broadleaf trees such as maples and oaks are ________ .
6. Trees continue to ________ as long as they live.

Reptiles

Reptiles include alligators, crocodiles, lizards, snakes, turtles and tuataras. Reptiles are cold-blooded, which means their body temperature is about the same as their surroundings. In climates with harsh winters they hibernate. In extremely hot climates they are mainly active at night. Many reptiles live a long time. Some turtles have lived in captivity for more than 100 years. Reptiles live on every continent except Antarctica, and in all the oceans except those in the polar regions. Some reptiles, including lizards, snakes and crocodiles, are hunted for their skins. The government prohibits the import of skins of those reptiles classified as endangered species.

backbone
dinosaur
land
lungs
plates
reptiles
shell
temperature

Across

2. Reptiles breathe air through ________ .
5. Cold-blooded animals do not have a constant body ________ .
7. A spectacular reptile that is now extinct ________ .
8. Most reptiles live on ________ .

Down

1. Reptile skin is made of scales or bony ________ .
3. An animal that is a vertebrate has a ________ .
4. Turtles, snakes, lizards and crocodiles are all ________ .
6. Turtles are the only reptiles with a ________ .

Word Meaning

Find a word to match each clue. Write the words in the puzzle.

Across

4. speak very softly
5. make a loud cry
7. say funny things
8. talk in a friendly way

Down

1. talk over
2. say out loud
3. talk big
6. share news

brag
chat
discuss
joke
report
scream
speak
whisper

Oceans

There are five oceans that surround the continents. Three of the great world oceans, in order of size, are the Pacific, the Atlantic and the Indian. These three oceans meet around the continent of Antarctica in the Southern Hemisphere to form the Antarctic Ocean. These three oceans meet again at the top of the earth to form the Arctic Ocean. The word **sea** can name any body of water, from a large lake to an ocean. Connected to each ocean are smaller bodies of water called seas, bays and gulfs that are defined by land or islands.

Across

3. These are places off a coast where seaweed grows as tall as trees _______ .
6. This fish doesn't look like one.
8. Seaweed doesn't have _______ to take in water.
9. You'll find the most colourful fish here.

Down

1. These form when wind blows across the ocean.
2. This fish looks like its name and stays near the ocean floor.
4. When the tide goes out, ocean water is left here.
5. Skeletons of these tiny animals form coral reefs.
7. The moon and sun cause the _______ .

Food Groups

A balanced diet is important for good nutrition. Nutrition is the science that deals with food and how the body uses it. There are five major food groups that nutrition experts recommend: (1) breads, cereals, rice and pasta; (2) vegetables; (3) fruits; (4) milk, yoghurt and cheese; and (5) meat, poultry, fish, dried beans and peas, eggs and nuts. Fats and sweets should be eaten in small quantities. A good diet helps prevent certain diseases and supplies the body with the energy needed to perform every action we make. The body needs good nutrition to help maintain all its functions and regulate the body processes.

Across

5. You get energy from these in bread, rice and potatoes.
6. This liquid is good for strong bones and teeth.
7. This is another word for carbohydrates.
8. This oily substance gives you energy and keeps you warm.
9. This comes from sea water and is sometimes added to food.
10. Spaghetti is one kind.

Down

1. It makes food sweet, but too much can cause cavities.
2. These come from plants, often taste sweet and are good to eat every day.
3. A kind of food that has protein you need to grow.
4. You should eat several servings a day from this food group.

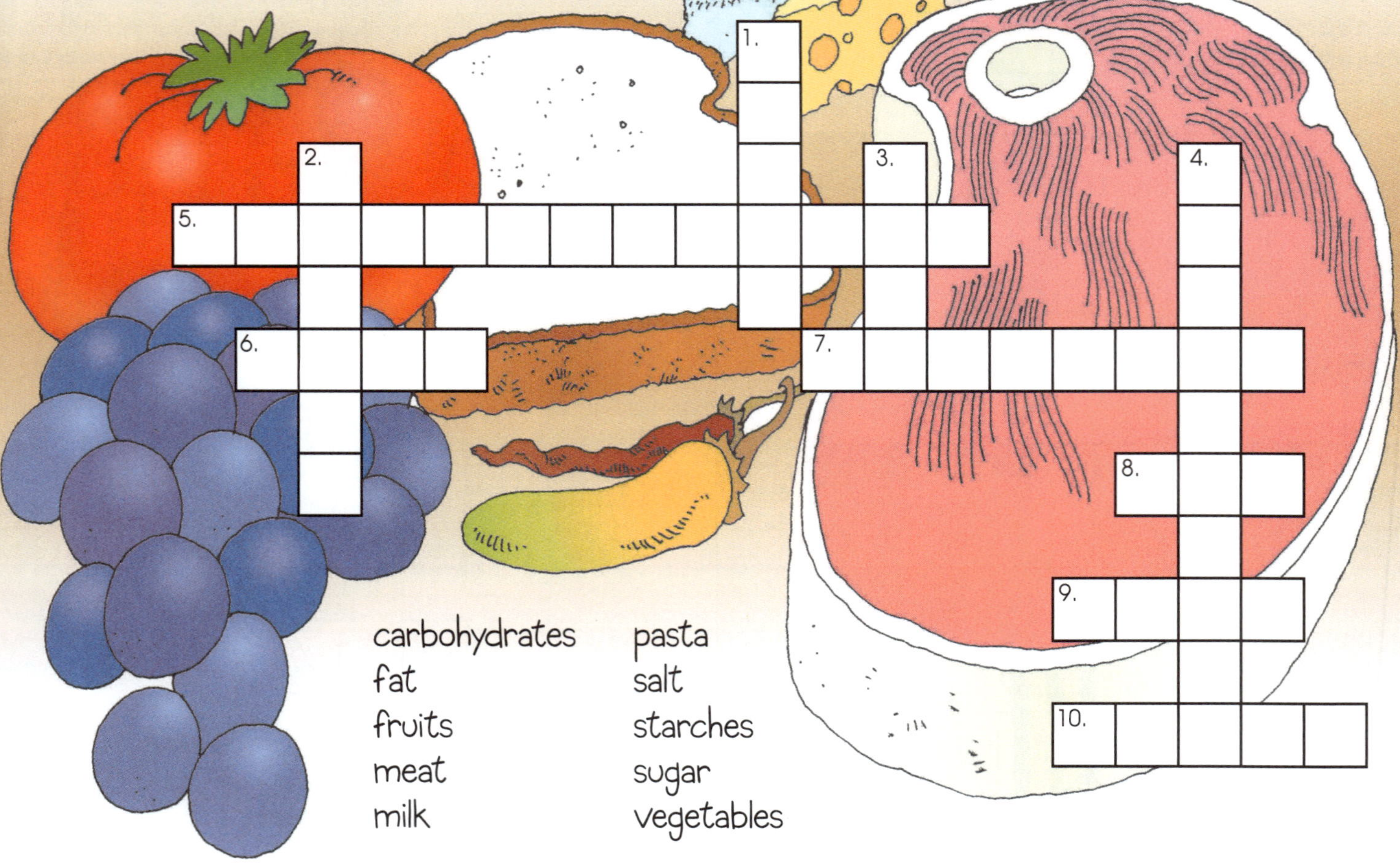

Bees

Bees are one of the most useful insects. During food-gathering, bees spread pollen from one flower to another. Many food crops, including fruits and vegetables, depend on bees for fertilization. They also produce honey, which people use as food, and beeswax that is used in candles, cosmetics and other products. They live in almost every part of the world except the North and South Poles.

drones
flowers
hives
honey
honeycomb
insects
queen's
sting
worker

Across

3. The ______ is used to raise young bees and to store nectar.
6. ______ provide food for bees.
8. Bees are ______ .

Down

1. The only function of the ______ is to mate with queens.
2. The job of the ______ honey bees is to collect nectar and pollen from flowers.
3. Only the kinds known as ______ bees make honey in large enough amounts to be used by people.
4. Honey bees live in ______ in a colony made up of one queen, tens of thousands of workers and a few hundred drones.
5. Laying eggs is the ______ only job.
7. Most bees depend on their ______ for defence.

Mammals

Mammals differ from most other animals in five important ways. Mother mammals feed milk from their own bodies to their young. Only mammals have hair for part or all of their lives. Mammals are warm-blooded. The temperature of their body stays the same no matter how hot or cold the weather. Mammals have a larger, more well-developed brain than other animals. Mammals care for their young. They protect them and teach them the skills they will need to live on their own. There are more than 4,500 species of mammals and they live almost everywhere.

bat
cat
cheetah
elephant
elk
fox
giraffe
goat
hippo
horse
rabbit
raccoon
whale
wolf
zebra

Across

1. longest neck
5. flying mammal
6. a kind of deer
7. a cowboy rides one
9. feline pet
10. looks like a striped horse
11. scared Red Riding Hood
13. third largest land animal

Down

1. Billy Goat Gruff was one
2. Peter is a well-known one
3. carries a trunk
4. the blue one is the largest mammal
8. wears a mask
9. fastest running animal for short distances
12. known as sly

1.
2.
3.
4.
5.
6.
7.
8.
9.
10.
11.
12.
13.

Homes

Write the words in the puzzle. Then circle the words on the list that name different kinds of home words.

apartment
cabin
castle
cottage
door
floor
houseboat
igloo
roof
teepee
walls

Habitats

The place where an animal lives is called its habitat. There are seven major types of habitats: mountains, grasslands, temperate forests, tropical forests, deserts, polar regions and oceans. Each habitat supports many kinds of animals. Most of these animals have lived in the same surroundings for centuries and have adapted to the climate. No single species of animal can survive everywhere. Habitats that are being destroyed, such as the rainforest, cause the death of many animals as they have lost their homes and source of food. Living things depend on one another. If all the trees in an area are cut down, the animals that depend on them will die.

Across

2. The ______ ______ exist in very hot and humid parts of the world where the temperature is relatively constant.
4. Plants and animals that live in the ocean live in ______.
8. An ______ is home to fish and mammals.
10. Marshes, bogs and swamps are all kinds of ______.

Down

1. ______ are wide areas covered with grasses and trees.
3. A ______ is a very dry place that receives very little rainfall and can support little vegetation. Not all are hot.
5. The ______ is a huge treeless plain that reaches from the Arctic Ocean to where the northern forests begin.
6. A deciduous ______ has trees that shed their leaves in autumn.
7. Most lakes, rivers and ______ are fresh water.
9. ______ are wetlands that are flooded all the time.

Circus

Circus-type performers go back thousands of years. In ancient Rome, part of the entertainment featured chariot races with men standing on the bare backs of two horses racing around the track. During the Middle Ages, jesters and other performers entertained on the streets or royal courts. The golden age of circuses in America began about 1870. A variety of performers, including aerialists, acrobats, clowns, dancers, musicians and trained animals, performed under a tent called the Big Top. Today, most circuses are held in tents and arenas around the world.

acrobats
band
Big Top
clowns
costumes
elephants
horses
jugglers
parade
rings
roustabouts
tigers
trapeze
tricks

Across

2. ______ wear bright velvet or satin ornaments and may have a pretty girl perched on their heads. Many are taught to do tricks.
5. ______ perform stunts, sometimes while on a cantering horse.
8. Aerialists perform while on a high ______ .
9. Trained ______ canter while riders jump from one to another.
10. ______ use a variety of objects such as dishes or even flaming torches.
11. ______ unload equipment, set it up and take it down after the last performance.
13. Circuses once took place under a tent called the ______ ______ .

Down

1. The circus ______ plays throughout the performance and sets the tempo for the acts.
3. Some circuses have a ______ where performers and animals march around the arena.
4. Different acts take place at the same time in different ______ .
6. All circus performers wear bright ______ .
7. ______ in funny costumes and comic makeup entertain the audience with playful antics and tricks.
8. ______ perform tricks while inside a wire cage with their trainer.
12. Both animals and clowns perform entertaining ______ .

1.
2.
3.
4.
5.
6.
7.
8.
9.
10.
11.
12.
13.

Ball Games

Across

3. Ping-Pong
5. not hardball
6. tenpins
9. pointy ball

Down

1. hands only
2. through the hoop
3. what a racket
4. not a vegetable
6. fast ball
7. putter around
8. heads up

baseball
basketball
bowling
football
golf
soccer
softball
squash
table tennis
tennis
volleyball

Cold Weather Mammals

Animals that live in icy conditions have evolved in different ways to cope. Mammals such as the polar bears have thick coats of long, shaggy hair and a fleecy layer of fur closer to their skin. Whales, polar bears and seals have thick layers of fat under their skin. Birds that live in polar regions have thick plumage and fluff out their feathers to help keep them warm. To be able to walk across the snow easily, bears have developed big, wide feet that act like snowshoes and birds such as ptarmigan and grouse have feathers on the soles of their feet. Animals that live in the polar regions are in sub-zero temperatures and total darkness for up to nine months during winter.

Across

3. Layers of ______ help keep some mammals warm.
5. The white bear of the frozen Arctic is called the ______ ______ .
7. Walrus ______ is tough and waterproof.
9. The mountain goat's hoofs are ______ on the bottom.
10. The polar bear uses its ______ legs to pull itself through the water.

Down

1. A mammal with tusks that is related to seals is the ______ .
2. Thick ______ keeps some mammals warm.
4. Mountain sheep and goats have sharp ______ .
6. Some mammals sleep all winter, or ______ .
8. In the Arctic, temperatures below ______ are not unusual.

Board Games

There is a great variety of board games, and each year many new board games appear on the market. Both children and adults enjoy games, whether for the challenge of perfecting a skill, the excitement of competition or simply for fun. One of the oldest known board games has been dated by archaeologists to be 4500 years old. Some board games require skill and strategy, and some are games of chance. Board game categories include trivia games, word games, games of logic and deduction, and financial games.

Across

2. strategy game known to be at least 4300 years old and very popular in China, Japan and Korea
3. game based on knowledge of an array of subjects
4. detective game
5. one of the oldest strategy games played to capture the opponent's king
7. child's game of chance where you can climb up or slide down with a roll of the dice.

Down

1. game using play money to buy and sell real estate
4. game similar to chess, the object of which is to capture the opponent's men
6. word game that requires spelling and vocabulary skills

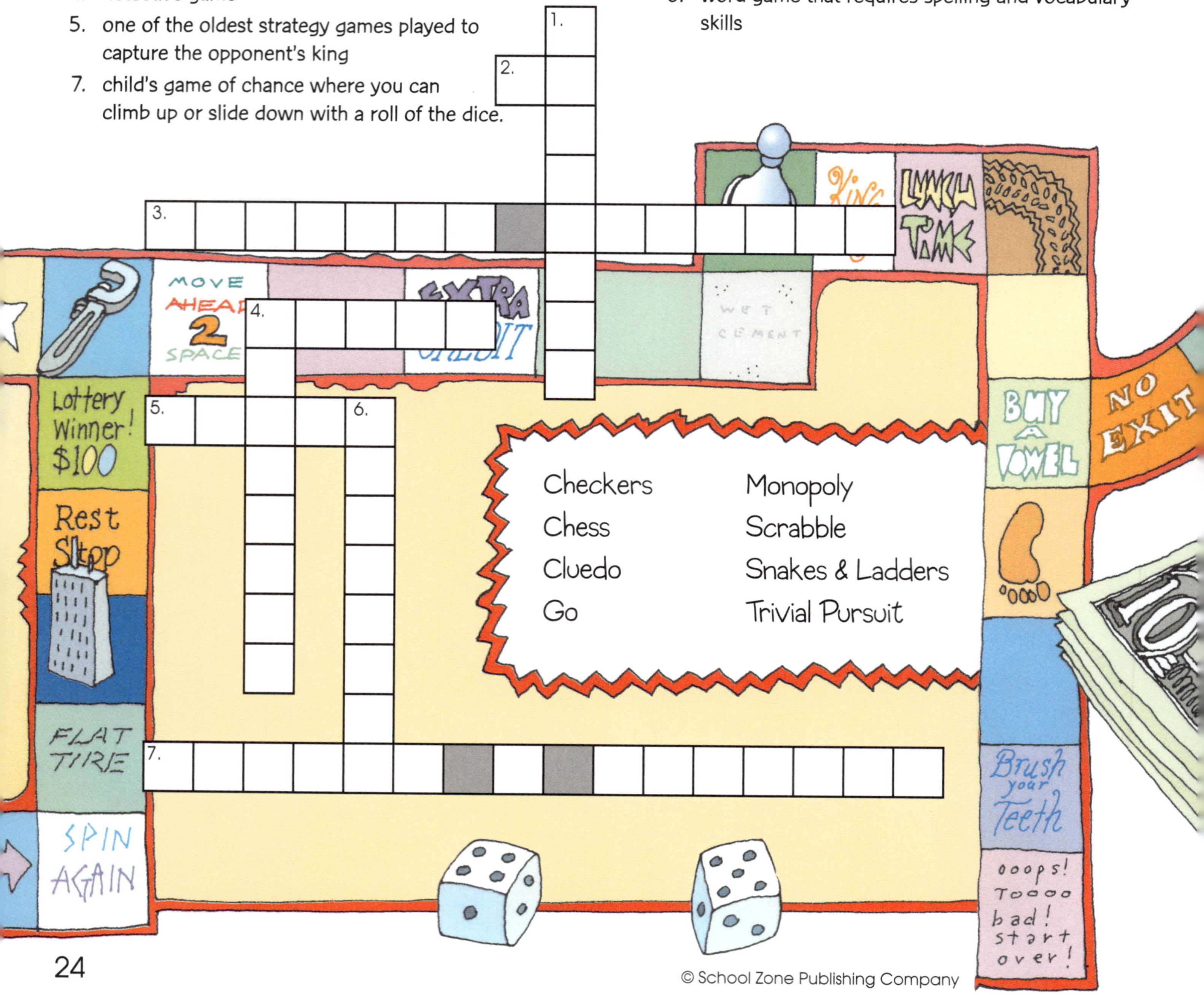

Checkers
Chess
Cluedo
Go
Monopoly
Scrabble
Snakes & Ladders
Trivial Pursuit

Sports

Sports are organised athletic activities played by individuals or in teams. Sports are played for fun, exercise or competition. There are different types of sports. Individual sports do not require a group or team of players. Combative sports set one person against another as in boxing. Outdoor sports such as camping involve people in nature. Team sports, including football and basketball, require players to communicate and work together. Many people participate in amateur sports such as organised basketball leagues. Professional athletes participate in sports as careers.

Across

1. downhill slide
3. it's a kick
5. love for two
7. batter up
9. curved sticks
10. small ball

Down

1. free wheeling
2. dunk it
4. down the alley
6. full forward
8. against the wall

Natural Disasters

Natural disasters are sudden and extremely unfortunate events that affect many people. Meteorologists study weather and the earth to predict and understand natural disasters. Different parts of the world have different kinds of disasters. Avalanches are huge drifts of snow that rush downward. Volcanoes erupt hot gases and melted rock from kilometres below the earth's surface. Tornadoes, hurricanes and typhoons are caused by tremendous winds. Earthquakes result from moving plates deep in the earth. Tsunamis are huge ocean waves caused by undersea earthquakes or volcanoes.

avalanche
blizzard
cyclones
earthquake
flood
hurricane
tornado
tsunami
typhoons

Across

3. a huge downward drift of snow
5. violent, rotating winds that form a funnel cloud that can destroy almost everything in its path when it touches ground
7. a violent motion of the earth's surface caused by volcanoes or rock movement below the earth's surface
8. a powerful storm that develops over warm water with a calm area in the centre and winds that swirl around the eye

Down

1. hurricanes near Australia and in the Indian Oceans are called _______
2. a blinding snowstorm with strong, cold winds
4. the overflow of water on land where people live caused by too much rain or melting snow
5. huge ocean waves caused by undersea earthquakes or volcanoes
6. hurricanes are called _______ in the Western Pacific Ocean and South China Seas

Sea Mammals

Until 1758, whales were regarded as fish. Though resembling some of the large sharks, they have all the attributes of mammals. They breathe air with lungs, they give birth to living young that are nursed on the mother's milk and they guard their young. Whales are found in all oceans. Walruses inhabit only the Arctic Ocean and adjacent ice-covered seas. In the quest for their ivory tusks and thick hide for oil, Europeans nearly eliminated the walrus from the Arctic almost 100 years ago. Seals generally live along the continental coasts and islands. Most types of seals live in the earth's polar and temperate zones, where fish populations are largest.

blowhole
blue
mammals
salt
seals
steer
surface
walrus
water

Across

2. Ocean water is ______ water.
3. Whales use flippers to balance and ______ .
5. Whales and dolphins are ______ .
7. Dolphins breath out a ______ .
8. Sea lions and ______ spend much of their life in water.

Down

1. Over two-thirds of Earth is covered by ______ .
3. Dolphins and whales come to the ______ to breathe.
4. Scientists classify the ______ as a kind of large seal.
6. The ______ whale is the largest animal on Earth.

Inventors

Inventing is putting ideas and materials together to make something that did not exist before. Inventions have been occurring since the Stone Age when people began using rocks as tools. New inventions can make life easier, healthier, more comfortable and fun.

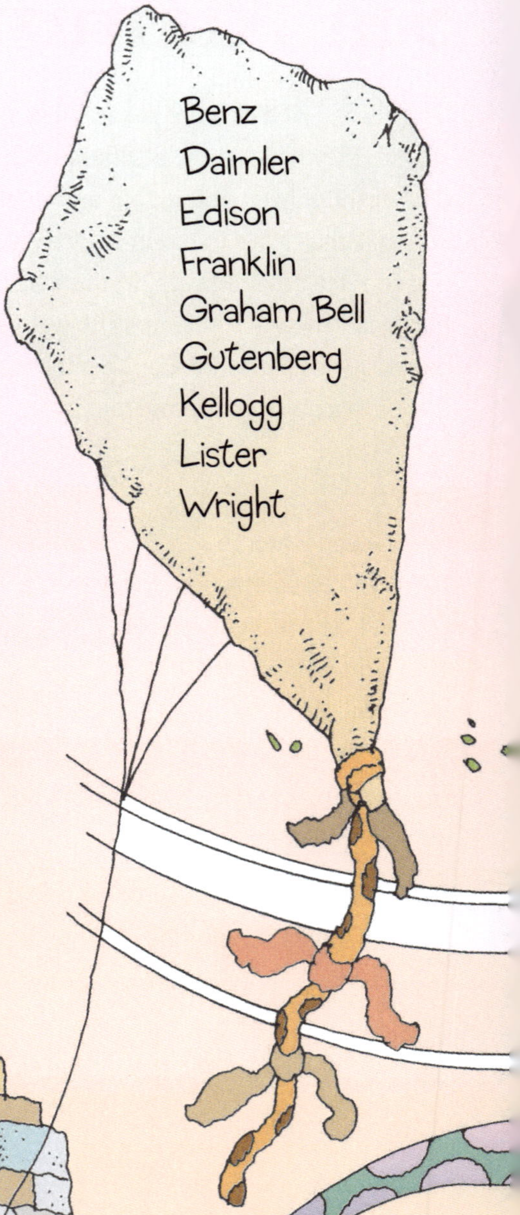

Across

3. In the mid 1400s, Johannes ______ invented printing as we know it today.
5. In 1865, Joseph ______ began the use of antiseptics during surgery, which almost eliminated post-surgical infection.
6. The electric light bulb was invented by Thomas ______ in the late 1800s.
7. A breakfast cereal still produced today was developed by Will ______ in the 1890s.

Down

1. The ______ brothers are credited with the first real aeroplane flights in 1903.
2. In 1885, Karl ______ and Gottlieb ______ built the first internal-combustion engines that were basically the same as the petrol engines used in cars today.
3. Alexander ______ ______ patented the telephone in 1876.
4. In 1752, Benjamin ______ flew a kite in a thunderstorm to prove lightning was electrical, which led to his invention of the lightning rod.

1.
2.
3.
4.
5.
6.
7.

Seeing Double

Some words have more than one meaning. There are two clues for each word in the puzzle. Think of a word that fits both clues. Write the word in the puzzle.

file
plant
ball
kind
pound
hand
light
play
rattle

Across

4. not heavy
   to set on fire
5. to conveniently arrange papers a tool with ridges used
   to smooth surfaces
7. an enclosure where stray animals are kept until redeemed
   to hit with a heavy blow
8. a big dance
   a round object used in sports

Down

1. a warning sound made by a kind of snake
   a baby's toy that makes noise when shaken
2. a herb, tree or shrub
   to put in the ground so that it will grow
3. friendly, generous
   sort or variety
6. part of the body at the end of the arm
   to pass or give something to someone
7. to have fun
   a story that is acted out on a stage

Try saying the tongue twisters below and then write some of your own!

Wood said he would carry the wood through the woods. And if Wood said he would, Wood would.

Garden Maths Puzzle

Solve the problems. Write the answers in the puzzle.

Across

A. 12 more than 10

B. 90, 95, 100, _____

C. 14 + 15 = _____

D. 8 + 9 = _____

E. 19 – 7 = _____

F. 3, 6, 9, _____

G. 120 – 15 = _____

H. 2 tens, 8 ones

I. 50¢ + 35¢ = _____

J. 29 – 13 = _____

Down

A. 284 + 12 = _____

B. 27 – 8 = _____

C. 2 hundreds, 2 tens, 2 ones

D. 5, 10, _____

E. one dozen

F. 2 x 9 = _____

G. 3 x 5 = _____

H. 2 hundreds, 3 tens, 6 ones

I. $1.00 – 15¢ = _____

Birds

If it has feathers, it's a bird. All birds have feathers and all birds have wings. But not all birds fly. Ostriches walk or run and penguins use their wings for balance when they walk or as flippers when they swim. Birds hatch from eggs. There are about 9700 kinds of birds. The fastest birds can fly at speeds over 160 kilometres an hour. No other animal can travel faster than birds. Birds are important to man in many ways. They scatter seeds, pollinate flowers, eat harmful insects and are an important source of food for people. Birds live all over the world, from the polar regions to the tropics.

cones
down
frogs
hummingbirds
molt
oil
straight
toes

Across

4. Birds have ______ that keeps their feathers dry.
5. These birds can fly backward.
8. Ostriches have two big ______ .

Down

1. Herons eat fish and ______.
2. These feathers keep birds warm.
3. The bottom of a bird's wing is ______.
6. When birds ______, they lose feathers a few at a time.
7. Seed-eating birds have beaks shaped like this.

Eat Right!

Use the clues to solve the puzzle.

vegetables
sugar
starches
fruits
milk
pasta
salt
meat
fat
carbohydrates

Across

5. You get energy from these in bread, rice and potatoes.
6. This liquid is good for strong bones and teeth.
7. another word for carbohydrates
8. an oily substance that gives you energy and keeps you warm
9. This comes from ocean water and is sometimes added to food.
10. Spaghetti is one kind.

Down

1. It makes food sweet, but too much can cause cavities.
2. These come from plants, often taste sweet and are good to eat every day.
3. one kind of food that has the protein you need to grow
4. These plants are grown for food. You should eat several servings a day.

Tennis

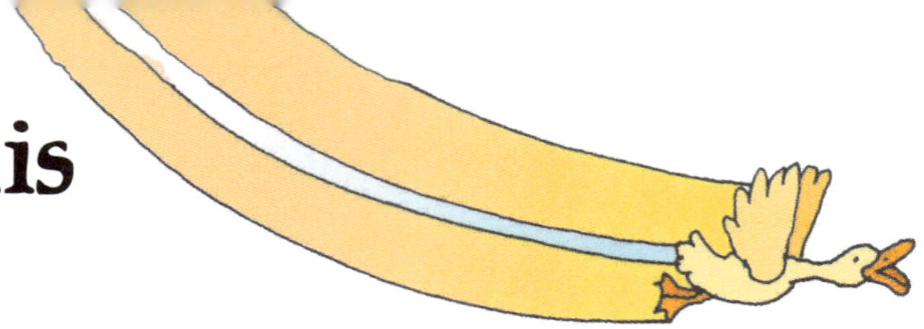

ace
ball
court
deuce
doubles
love
net
players
point
racket
service
set
singles

Across

1. Tennis is a game played with one or two opposing ______.
7. A ______ is used to hit the ball.
9. A zero score is called ______.
10. A game of ______ is played with four people.
11. To win a ______ a player or team must win six games and lead by at least two games.
12. A ______ is stretched across the middle of the court.

Down

1. A ______ is won when the opposing side fails to return the ball or makes an error.
2. A serve that cannot be returned is an ______.
3. ______ is a game played with two opposing people.
4. A 40-40 tie is called ______.
5. The ______ puts the ball in play.
6. Rackets are used to hit the ______ back and forth over a net.
8. Tennis is played on a flat surface called a ______.

Maths Vocabulary

Write the definitions of the items in red to solve the puzzle.

Across

b. $\begin{array}{r} 3 \\ 3\overline{)9} \end{array}$ d. $4/5$ g. $3/4$ h. $\begin{array}{r} 4 \\ 3\overline{)12} \end{array}$

i. $7 \times 8 = 56$ j. ⁙ ⁙ ⁙ k. $4 \times 6 = 24$

Down

a. $\begin{array}{r} 3 \\ +4 \\ \hline 7 \end{array}$ c. $9/10$ e. $\begin{array}{r} 3 \\ 3\overline{)10} \\ 9 \\ \hline 1 \end{array}$ f. $\begin{array}{r} 12 \\ -6 \\ \hline 6 \end{array}$ g. $\begin{array}{r} 9 \\ 2\overline{)18} \end{array}$

denominator
difference
dividend
divisor
factors
fraction
numerator
product
quotient
remainder
sets
sum

Name That Dog

People have had dogs as pets for over 10,000 years. Most scientists believe that prehistoric man first valued dogs as watchdogs. Dogs eventually became used for herding and hunting other animals. Over thousands of years, different breeds were developed for certain tasks. Some breeds were developed to herd sheep, goats and cattle. Others were bred for various kinds of hunting. Many kinds of toy dogs were developed to provide company for people. Dogs perform many important tasks for people. Police use dogs to track criminals and sniff out illegal drugs and hidden explosives. They also lead the blind and serve as 'ears' for deaf people. Many dogs have been trained to perform in circuses and in films.

Afghan
Beagle
Boxer
Dachshund
Dalmation
Great Dane
Greyhound
Husky
Pointer
Poodle
Retriever
Setter

Across

2. not a bus
6. go fetch dog
7. not a sitter
8. long, silky hair
10. does not wear gloves
11. dark spots

Down

1. looks like a wolf
2. BIG
3. sausage dog
4. points the way
5. rabbit chaser
9. fancy haircuts

43
DOG

Land Transportation

Land transportation is the most common kind of transportation by far. Cars, buses, motorcycles, trains and trucks are the chief engine-powered vehicles. Cars, buses and trucks are the main road vehicles. Routes are predetermined for buses, and trains and subways that run on tracks. Trucks can deliver freight to where it is needed. Cars allow people to choose their routes. Cars consume a large portion of the energy used for transportation and are a major source of traffic congestion and pollution problems in cities and towns. Many governments have established pollution-control standards and fuel-consumption standards to help reduce these problems.

car
bus
truck
tram
train
motorcycle
bicycle
taxi

Across

1. a large passenger vehicle
2. a vehicle designed to move heavy objects
3. a two-wheeled – sometimes with a third for a side car – automotive vehicle
4. a connected line of cars that ride on rails, pulled by a locomotive

Down

1. a two-wheeled vehicle propelled by pedalling
2. rides on rails and transports passengers on city streets
5. a chauffeur-driven car for hire
6. a vehicle by which most families travel

HONEST JONATHAN'S
USED VEHICLES
ONE OWNER CREAM PUFF
1.
2.
3.
4.
5.
6.

Airports

Across

1. people who buy tickets to travel by plane
3. where air traffic controllers direct air traffic near the airport and movement on the ground
6. paper that shows you have paid and where you are going
7. buildings in which aircraft are stored and repaired
8. where passengers board and leave aircraft from terminal locations
10. what must be inspected by security employees

Down

1. a person qualified to operate an aeroplane
2. enforce security regulations
4. roads for planes to take off and land
5. the main airport building for passengers and services
9. provides energy and power to engines

baggage
control tower
fuel
gate
hangars
passengers
pilot
runways
security guards
terminal
tickets

Shape Words

Write the names of the figures in the puzzle.

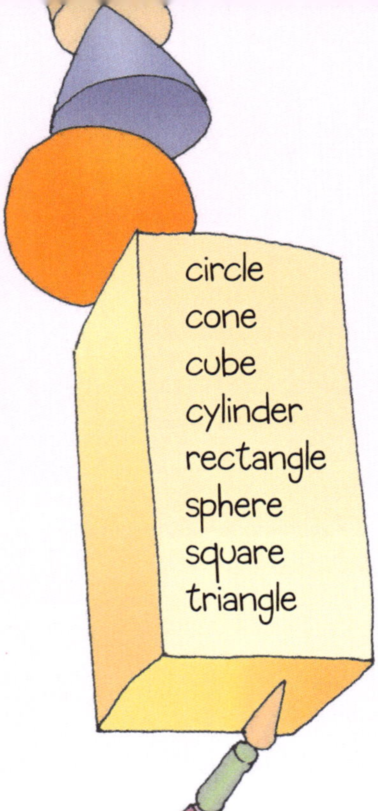

Across

5. 

6. 

7. 

8. 

Down

1. 

2. 

3. 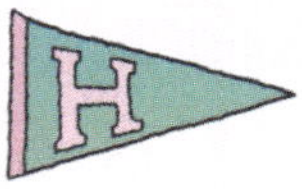

4. 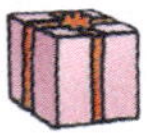

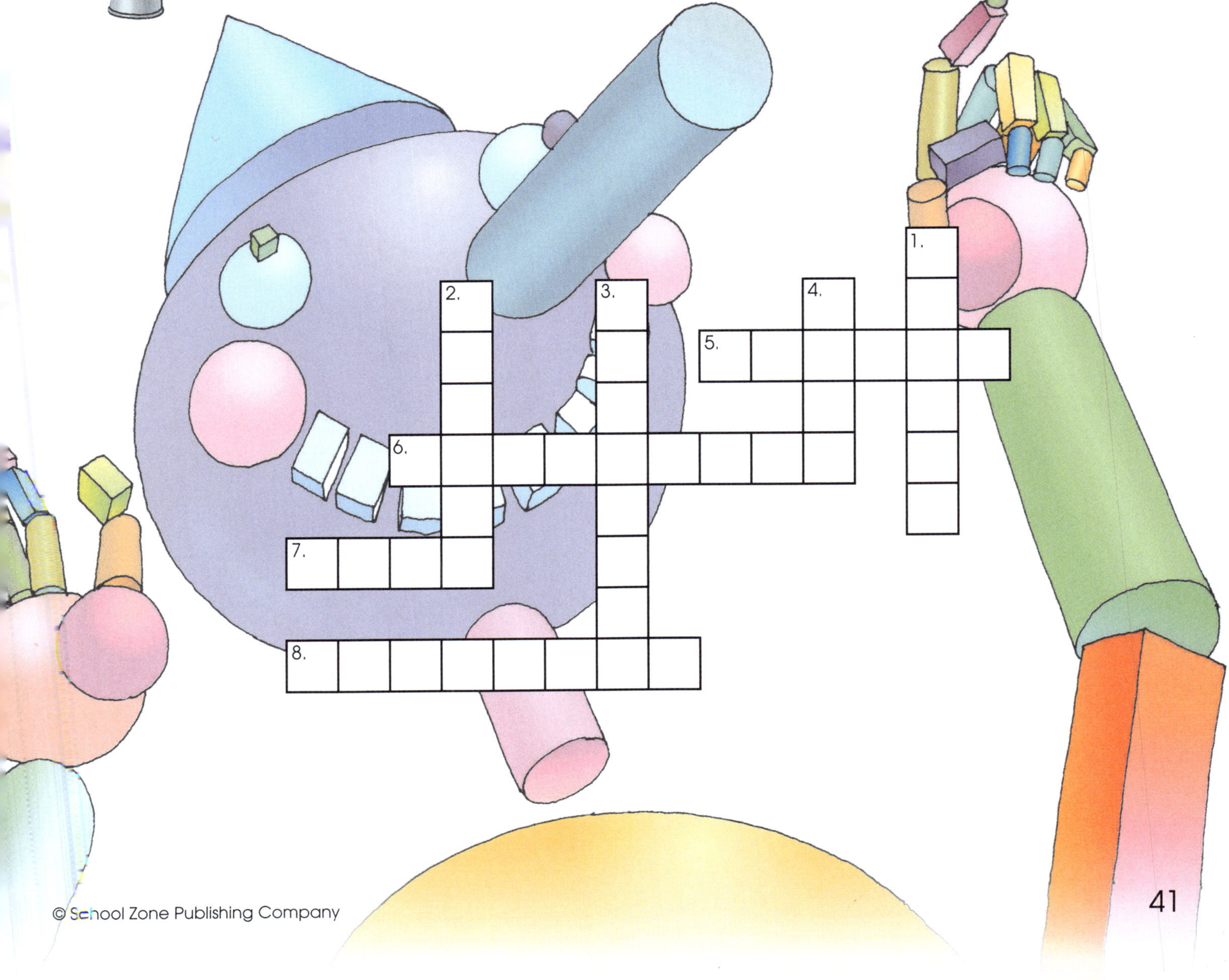

Bad Guys

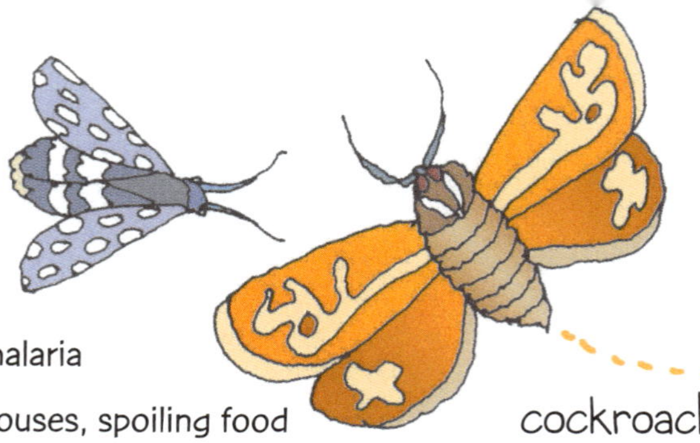

Across

1. a bloodsucking insect that carries diseases such as malaria
3. an insect that invades homes, restaurants and warehouses, spoiling food
5. a kind of bat that drinks the blood of warm-blooded animals
6. pests that live in the fur of dogs and cats
9. caterpillars of this insect strip leaves from trees, killing many of them

cockroach
fleas
gypsy moth
housefly
mosquito
rat
scorpion
termites
vampire

Down

2. an arachnid that has a poisonous sting in its tail
4. a common, winged pest that invades homes and can carry diseases such as typhoid fever
7. these ant-like insects eat wood in our homes and can cause great damage
8. a rodent that carries diseases and will attack humans

What Makes Weather?

Weather takes place in the atmosphere, the layer of air that surrounds the earth. Most weather occurs from the earth's surface up to an altitude of about ten to 16 kilometres. Three factors determine the weather. **Air temperature**, which is the measure of warmth; **air pressure**, which affects wind; and **humidity**, a measure of the amount of water vapour in the air. There are all kinds of weather – rain, snow, sun, wind, fog, frost. All of them are changes in the air caused by the varying effect of the sun's warmth. Winds blow, for instance, when the sun heats some places more than others, causing air to move. Rain falls when air warmed by the sun causes enough evaporation to form big drops of water when it condenses. Weather affects people's lives every day in all parts of the world.

air pressure
condensation
evaporation
precipitation
temperature
water
weather
wind

Across

1. A thermometer measures ________ .
3. What we wear depends on the ________ .
7. Rain, snow and hail are kinds of ________ .
8. Drops of water on a cold can are ________ .

Down

2. ________ is what happens when water turns to water vapour.
4. The push of air on the earth is ________ ________ .
5. Cold air can't hold as much ________ as warm air can.
6. Moving air is ________ .

Rodents

Rodents are mammals with front teeth especially suited to gnawing hard objects. Rodents have two top and two bottom front teeth. They wear away at the tips but do not wear out until late in the animal's lifetime as they keep growing until the animal becomes old. There are many kinds of rodents. They are both helpful and harmful to people. Scientists use mice and rats for research. Some rodents eat harmful insects and weeds. Beavers, chinchillas and other rodents have valuable fur. But serious diseases, such as typhus and the plague, are carried by rodents. Some rodents cause damage to crops and property.

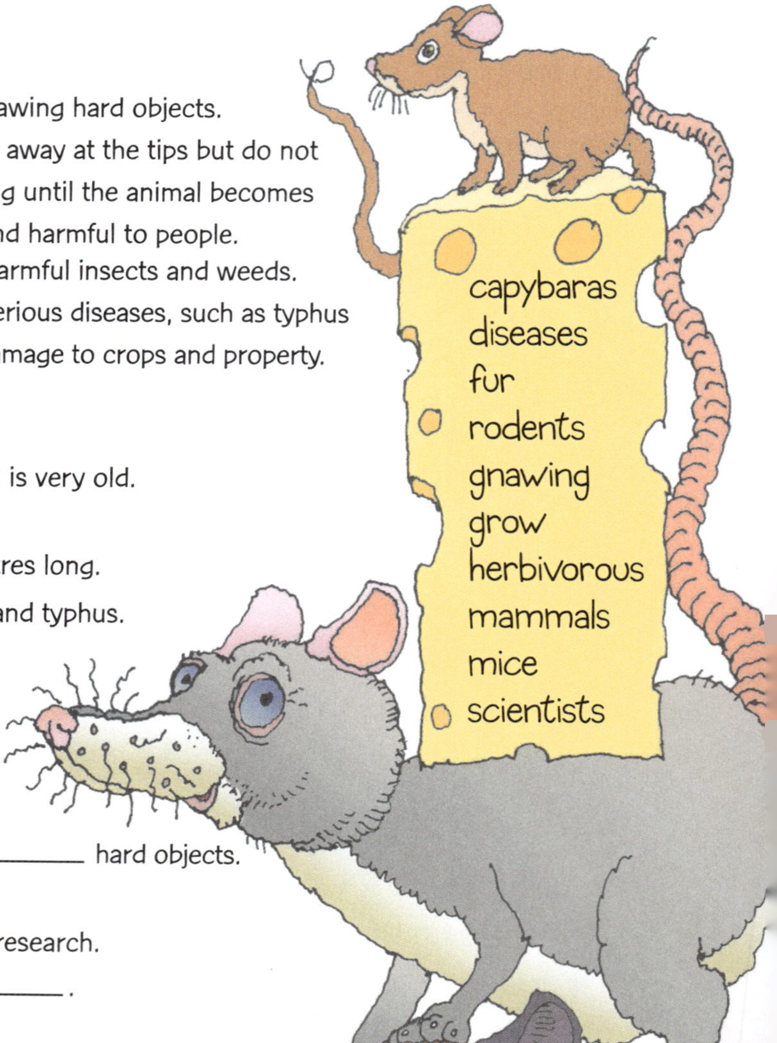

Across

1. The teeth of rodents continue to _______ until the animal is very old.
2. Rodents are _______.
4. _______ are the largest rodents and can be up to 1.2 metres long.
5. Many rodents carry serious _______ such as the plague and typhus.
6. _______ live in almost all parts of the world.
8. Most rodents are _______ (plant eaters).

Down

1. A rodent is an animal with front teeth especially suited to _______ hard objects.
2. _______ are the smallest rodents.
3. Rats and mice are helpful to _______, who use them for research.
7. Some rodents such as chinchilla rabbits have valuable _______.

Baseball

Across

2. A _________ throws the ball for the player at bat.
6. The approximate shape of the infield is a _________ .
7. A _________ is a long, rounded wooden stick used to hit the ball.
8. Home plate has ________ sides.
9. An _________ calls balls and strikes.
11. Each _________ marks a corner of the diamond that runners must touch to score a run.
12. The _________ is the area of the baseball field that is outside the infield.
13. Defensive players wear a _________ on one hand.

Down

1. A _________ is called when a batter swings and misses.
3. The batter stands at _________ plate.
4. A player who moves from third base to cross home plate scores a _________ .
5. A _________ catches the balls that pass the batter.
8. A ball that is batted high into the air is called a _________ .
10. An _________ is a division of the game in which both teams have a turn at bat and in the field.
12. A team's turn at bat is over after three _________ .

base
bat
catcher
diamond
five
fly ball
glove
home
inning
outfield
outs
pitcher
run
strike
umpire

Ecosystems

Different parts of the world support a wide variety of plant and animal life. This is mainly caused by the climate in each place, which allows different kinds of living things to thrive. The climate is influenced by the physical characteristics of a region – whether it is mountainous or near the sea, for example – and its position on Earth. Similar conditions exist in different parts of the world even if they are thousands of kilometres apart. Each area contains communities of living things that rely on each other for survival. These communities are called ecosystems.

Across

2. An animal that eats flesh of another animal is a ______.
4. Evaporation, condensation and precipitation are the three steps to the ______ ______.
6. The environment in which a species lives.
7. ______ is the study of how plants and animals interact.
8. An animal that eats plants is a ______.
9. Animals that eat both plants and animals are ______.
10. The study of plants is called ______.

Down

1. A ______ is a plant or animal that lives in or on another plant or animal for its only source of food.
3. ______ is the science of weather.
5. Plants and animals need water and ______ to live.

botany
carnivore
ecology
habitat
herbivore
meteorology
omnivores
oxygen
parasite
water cycle

Body Systems

The human body has nearly a dozen interrelated systems, each designed for a special function. The skeleton is the framework. Bones provide the system for putting muscular contractions into bodily movements. Oxygen needed to provide fuel for muscles depends on the circulatory system that depends on the respiratory system, and so on with other related systems. Each part of our body does a special job, but all parts work together. What separates people from all other living things is the human brain. Everything you think, feel and do is controlled by the brain.

blood
brain
ears
eyes
heart
lungs
muscles
skeleton
skin

Across

1. ______ connect with the brain through the optic nerve and are one of our senses.
2. ______ hold and move the skeleton and give the body its shape.
4. The______ and blood circulation are the major elements of the body's internal transportation system.
5. ______ draw air into the body through the mouth and nose so that oxygen can be absorbed into the bloodstream.
7. The______ is an outgrowth at the top of the spinal cord and is the organ of thought and neural coordination.

Down

1. ______ are located at the sides of the head and are concerned with the senses of learning and balance.
3. The______ is the framework around which the body is built.
6. ______ is what the whole body is enclosed in and forms the body's largest organ.
7. ______ contains food, fuel and materials for building and repairing cells vital to every tissue of the body.

Great Inventions

Invention is the creation of a new device or process or product. It may be the creation of something new or an improvement of something that someone else had produced. Invention is closely related to discovery. Discoverers usually find something that has always existed. For example, people discovered fire, but they invented the match to start a fire. If we compare our homes today with the homes of pioneers, you will appreciate the many inventions that have made our lives easier. Inventions can be beneficial to people, but they can also be harmful. Weapons of war are far more destructive than they once were. People invent to satisfy the needs of people, to make money, or meet military needs. Many inventions fail because they do not fill a need.

aeroplane
camera
clock
computer
map
microscope
plough
printing press
satellite
telephone
television
wheel

Across

2. made possible mass communication before radio
3. brings pictures and sound from around the world
4. any body that revolves around a planet – artificial ones used for communication and research
5. a machine that processes information with great speed and precision
6. a reference, usually printed, to help people find a destination
7. the first one was probably a potter's table
8. used for taking photographs or making movies
9. an engine-driven machine that can fly

Down

1. an instrument that magnifies extremely small objects
2. a tool used to prepare soil for planting
3. an instrument that sends and receives sound, usually by electricity
5. an instrument that shows time

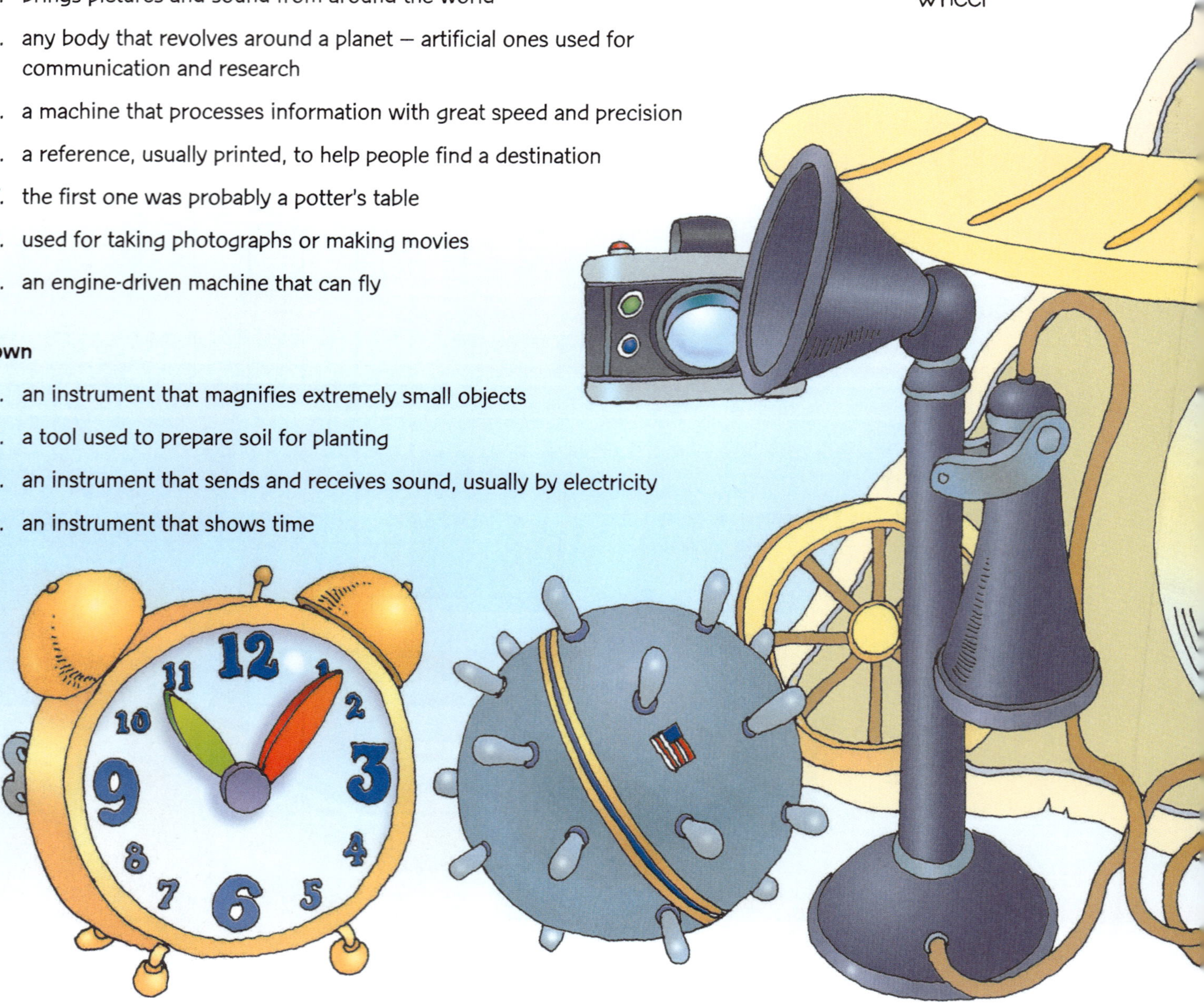

BOG
RUFFY ROAD
LAKE CLAMBAKE
BOBWILLY WOODS
SWAMP
1.
2.
3.
4.
5.
6.
7.
8.
9.

Our Sun

Across

1. When the magnetic field in the sun's core prevents heat from rising to the surface, these dark spots appear: _______ .
5. _______ is another word for star system.
6. There can be no _______ without the sun.
7. The sun shines because it gives out _______ and _______ .
10. Our sun is a type of star called a _______ _______ because it is small compared to other types and gives off a yellow light.

Down

1. _______ _______ are huge eruptions of flames that appear on the sun's surface.
2. A _______ is a huge ball of gas that gives off vast amounts of light and heat.
3. A star is made of _______ and has no solid surface.
4. Our galaxy is named the _______ _______ .
8. Light and heat are forms of _______ .
9. The centre of the sun is its _______ .

core
energy
galaxy
gas
light & heat
life
Milky Way
solar flares
star
sunspots
yellow dwarf

Parts of Speech

The eight ways in which words are used are called the eight parts of speech. A word must be used in a sentence before one can determine which part of speech it is.

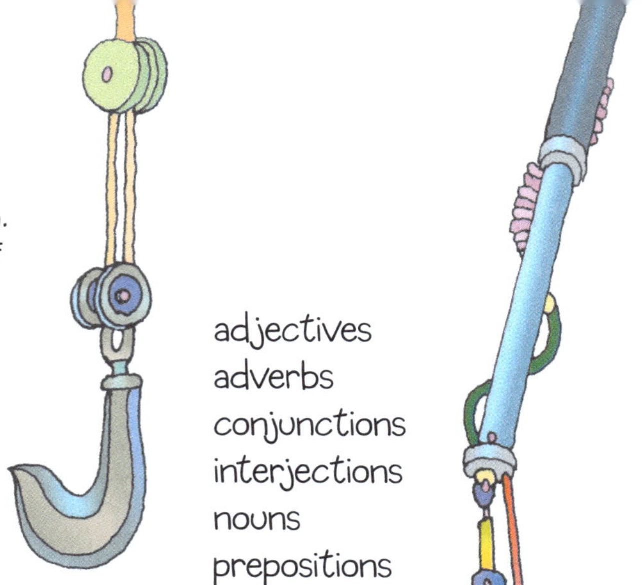

adjectives
adverbs
conjunctions
interjections
nouns
prepositions
pronouns
verbs

Across

2. _______ take the place of nouns.
5. _______ are the name of anything.
6. _______ express strong feeling.
7. _______ modify a verb, an adjective or another adverb.

Down

1. _______ connect words, phrases and clauses.
2. _______ show a relationship between its object and another word in the sentence.
3. _______ modify a noun or a pronoun.
4. _______ express action or a state of being.

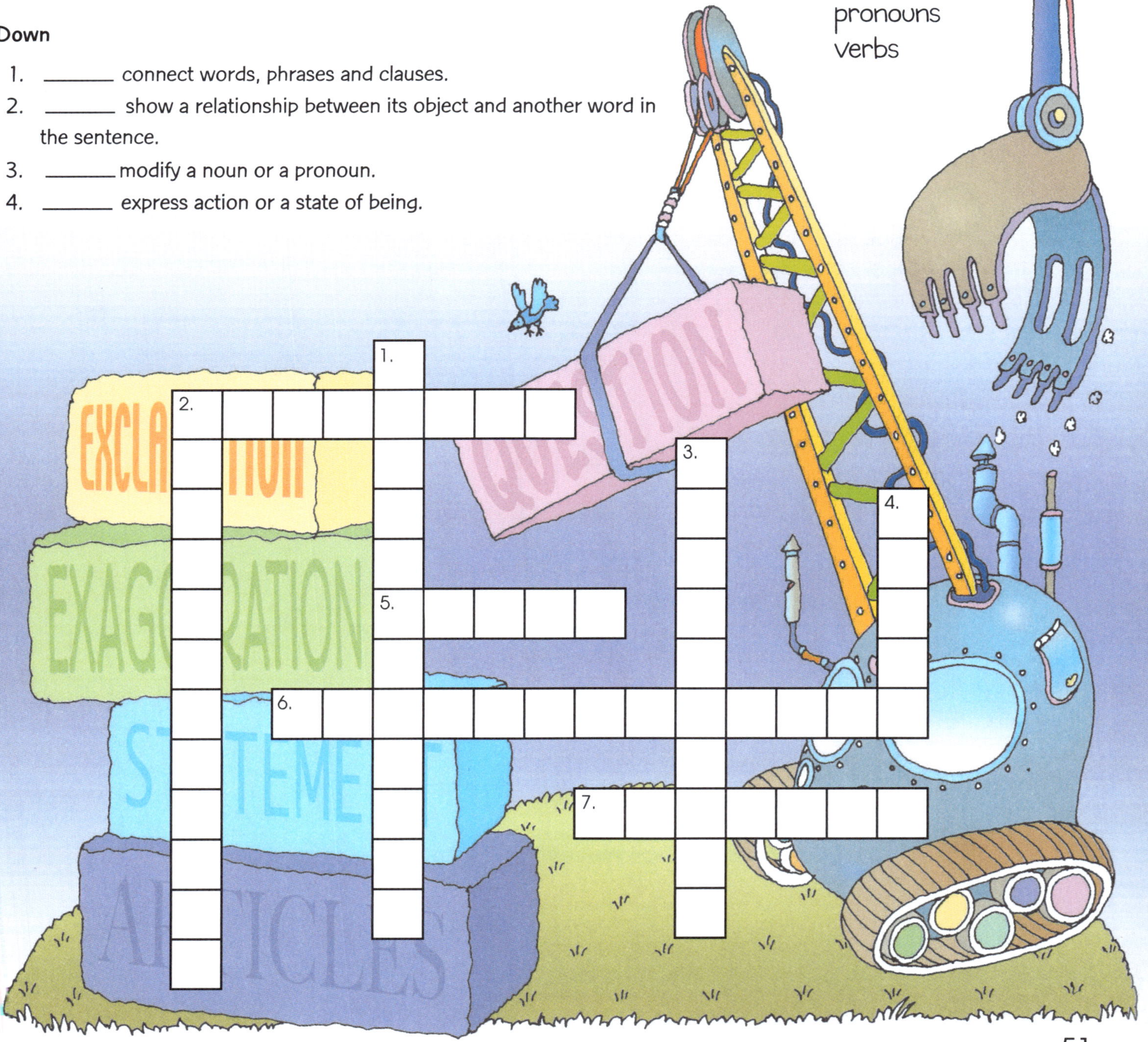

Raining Cats and . . .

Use the clues to solve the puzzle.

Down

1. Hurricanes form over ________ seas.
2. Lightning comes before ________ .
3. Heavy ________ comes with thunderstorms.
4. Thunderstorms come from fluffy ________ clouds.
7. Blizzards happen when the weather is very ________.

Across

5. This storm, which brings strong winds and heavy rain, forms over the ocean.
6. This cloud comes with a tornado.
8. A tornado is sometimes called a ________ .
9. This storm is the most violent kind and has swirling winds.
10. A cold, windy snowstorm is a ________ .

Green and Growing

Use the clues to solve the puzzle.

Across

3. We would starve without ________ from plants.
4. When we eat lettuce, we are eating these parts of the lettuce plant.
5. The ________ of plants grow underground.
7. There would be no ________ on Earth without plants.
8. Much of the ________ plants need to grow comes from rain.
10. Most plants need ________ to grow.
11. Dresses and other ________ can be sewn from fabric made from plants.
12. We eat them and sow them to grow crops.

Down

1. This is the process by which plants make their own food from air, sun and water.
2. When we're sick, we may take ________ made from plants.
4. rubbish that ruins our gardens and parks
6. Plants give us oxygen, food and ________ .
9. Plants take in carbon dioxide from the ________ .

Motion Pictures

Across

1. supervises the camera crew and lighting for the movie
2. turns a story or idea into a screenplay
3. chooses the director and creative team and controls the budget
5. nonfiction films that present factual information in a dramatic and entertaining way
8. designs and creates sets and oversees their construction
9. an award given for an outstanding achievement in film making

Down

1. designs and makes the costumes
4. guides the creative efforts of the screenwriter, cast and crew
6. a motion picture technique that creates the illusion of motion rather than recording it with a camera as live action
7. play the part of characters in a movie

actors
animation
art director
cinematographer
costume designer
director
documentaries
Oscar
producer
screenwriter

Geometry Crossword

Use the clues to write words from the word box to solve the crossword puzzle.

Across

4. A ________ line is not straight.
6. a four-sided figure with opposite sides the same length and parallel
8. a straight line where two faces meet
9. a solid shape with all points of the shape the same distance from the centre
11. a four-sided figure with only two parallel sides
12. It's straight, continues in both directions and doesn't end.
13. the figure formed by two straight lines that start at a single point

Down

1. A line of ________ divides a figure into matching halves.
2. the distance around a plane figure
3. a shape with six straight sides
5. figures that have the same size and shape are ________ .
7. the number of square units needed to cover a flat surface
9. Three-dimensional figures are ________ .
10. Its ________ is the flat surface of a solid figure.

Solar System

A solar system is made up of a star and the planets or other objects orbiting around it. Our solar system includes Earth and eight other planets that revolve around the sun, which is our star. In our solar system there are many smaller objects such as asteroids, meteoroids and comets. There is also a thin cloud of dust known as the interplanetary medium. More than 60 moons, also called satellites, orbit the planets. Astronomers have discovered planets orbiting distant stars and hope to learn more about our solar system by studying the masses and orbits of those systems.

Earth
Jupiter
Mars
Mercury
Moon
Neptune
Pluto
Saturn
Sun
Uranus
Venus

Across

2. the only planet whose surface can be seen in detail from Earth
3. a satellite of Earth whose light is reflected light from the sun, as it gives off no light of its own
4. has 15 moons and at least 11 rings around it discovered by photographs taken by the US Voyager 2 spacecraft
6. the second largest planet, encircled by seven major rings
8. the largest planet in our solar system
9. the most distant planet from the sun
10. the only planet known to support life

Down

1. known as the earth's 'twin' because the two planets are so similar in size
2. the nearest planet to the sun
5. a huge, glowing ball of gases at the centre of the solar system
7. named for the Roman god of the sea

1.
2.
3.
4.
5.
6.
7.
8.
9.
10.

Yellowstone National Park

Yellowstone National Park in the United States was established in 1872 and is the oldest national park in the world. The park occupies 8991 square kilometres in the northwestern corner of Wyoming and overlaps into Montana and Idaho. There is no other place of the same size that has as many natural wonders. Geysers, hot springs, sparkling lakes and rivers, and deep canyons attract over a million visitors a year. Yellowstone is the largest wildlife preserve in the United States. A large number of animals, including elk, deer, antelope, mountain sheep, buffalo, moose and grizzly bears, roam the park freely. The park is famous for some of the best fishing in the West, which is allowed under federal regulations.

Across

1. Volcanoes and ______ shaped the landscape of Yellowstone through millions of years.
4. Yellowstone Lake is the largest ______ ______ lake in North America.
5. Yellowstone Park is located mainly in ____.
7. Molten rock called ______ lies below the surface of the park and furnishes the heat for the park's geysers and hot springs.
9. In 1872, ______ passed a bill to establish the park and preserve its natural resources.

Down

2. The Yellowstone region was acquired in 1803 as part of the ______ ______.
3. The park's ______ forests were caused by lava ash during volcanic eruptions over 60,000 years ago.
6. Old Faithful is a famous ______ in the park.
8. The park was named for yellow ______ that lie along part of the Yellowstone River.

South America

Amazon
Andes
Angel Falls
Brazil
Colombia
Ecuador
Pampa
petroleum
rain

Across

1. Only the Nile River is longer than the ______ River that flows mainly through Brazil.
3. Venezuela is one of the world's leading producers and exporters of ______ , which has made the country one of the wealthiest on the continent.
5. ______ is the largest country in South America in both area and population.
6. The ______ mountains that stretch along Chile's eastern border are the world's longest mountain range above sea level.
8. ______ borders five other countries, the Pacific Ocean and the Caribbean Sea.

Down

1. ______ ______ in Venezuela has the longest drop of any other waterfall in the world.
2. The ______ is a fertile plain that covers about one fifth of Argentina and has some of the richest topsoil in the world.
4. More than one third of South America is covered by ______ forests.
7. ______ was named for the equator that crosses the country.

Architecture

Architects design more than one kind of structure. Houses, schools, stadiums and skyscrapers are a few of the many kinds that skilled builders have created throughout history. The Great Pyramid in Egypt was built some 4,500 years ago as a tomb. It was entirely solid, so an immense amount of stone was used to build it. In today's world, advances in engineering eliminate the need for heavy walls. Modern buildings can be much taller than those of the past, built of lightweight outer frameworks of steel and glass. Some of the world's tallest buildings are in cities where people live and work. Architecture is one of the oldest art forms, and many important works of architecture have survived for centuries.

Across

1. a large structure for spectators built around a field
3. a place where people go to be taught
4. the home fortress of a monarch
7. where medical services are provided

Down

1. an exceptionally tall building
2. where a collection of objects is displayed, many from the past
5. a place that provides overnight lodging for the public
6. a single building where people live, some big, some small

castle
hospital
hotel
house
museum
school
skyscraper
stadium

Rocks

To learn more about the earth's crust, geologists examine various rock samples. By using a microscope, they can study the different minerals that make up a rock's composition. Minerals are made up from atoms and molecules of different degrees of hardness. Diamond, the hardest, can cut glass. The hardness of a mineral is often used to identify it. All minerals came originally from the earth's hot interior, but at the surface they form three kinds of rock: sedimentary, metamorphic and igneous. Sedimentary rocks are formed in thin layers from materials that were part of older rocks or of plants and animals. Over millions of years, the mass is compressed by the weight of more sand and solidifies into sedimentary rock. Geologists can tell the age of a bed of sedimentary rock by examining the fossils that it contains. Metamorphic rock is made when other rock is altered by extreme heat or pressure. Ninety percent of the earth's crust is made from igneous rock formed from hot magma (molten rock) that wells up from the earth's interior. The materials rocks are made of are continually recycled to make new rocks in a process called the rock cycle.

Across

3. Atoms and molecules make up ______.
4. The hardest mineral is ______.
6. Geologists use a ______ to examine rocks.
8. Rocks that are formed in thin layers are ______ rock.

Down

1. Ninety percent of the earth's crust is made from ______ rock.
2. Minerals can be identified by their ______.
3. Heat and pressure change other rock into ______ rock.
5. The age of sedimentary rock can be determined by ______ found in it.
7. Igneous rock is formed from hot ______ rock.

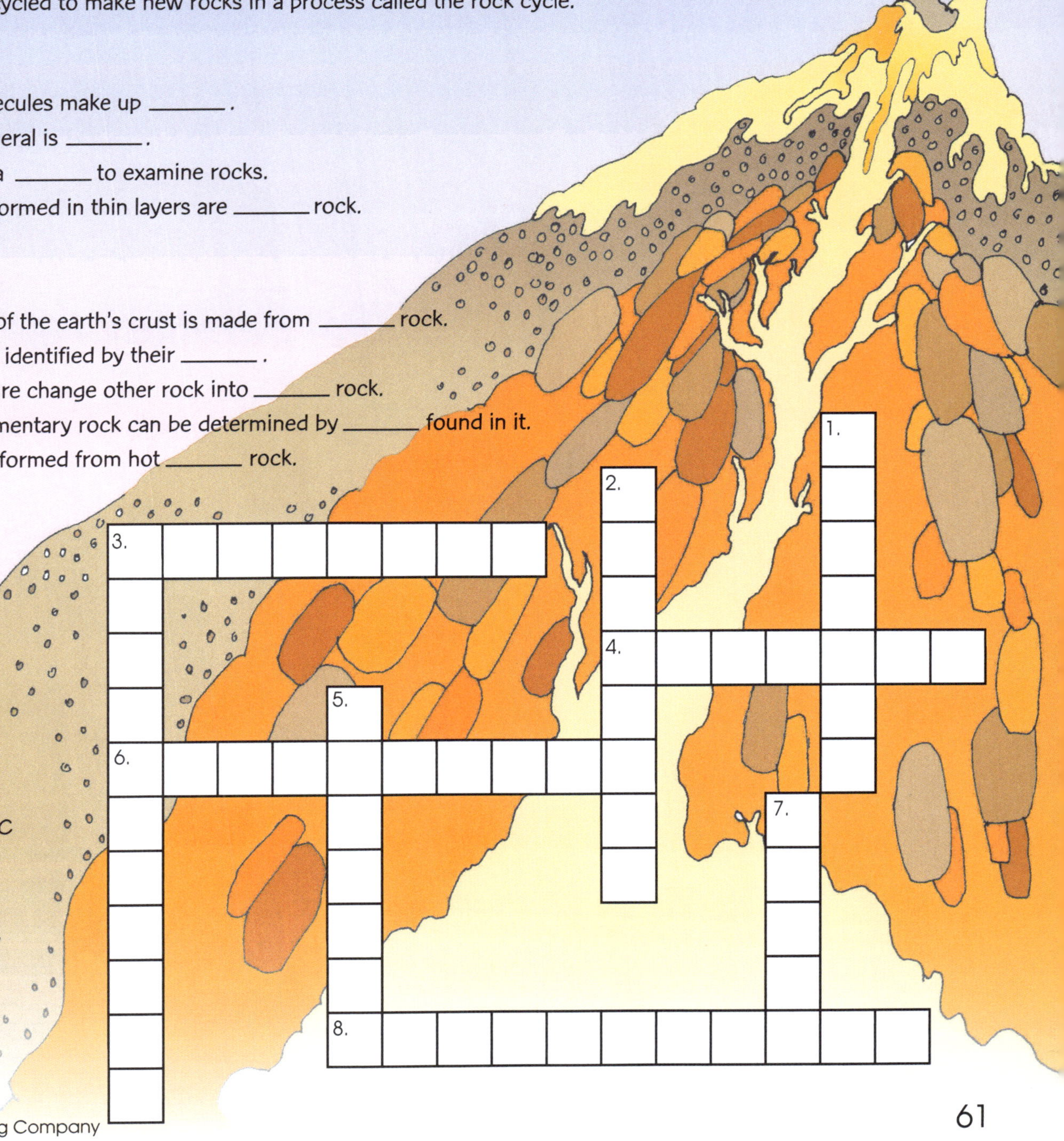

diamond
fossils
hardness
igneous
magma
metamorphic
microscope
minerals
sedimentary

Made by Nature or People?

Across

2. a public road
7. a landform that is much higher than its surroundings
8. a structure carrying a roadway over water or an obstacle
9. a dock or basin providing mooring for motorboats or yachts
10. a permanent road of rails providing a track for locomotives

Down

1. a large inland body of water
3. a tract of land surrounded by water and smaller than a continent
4. a very steep descent of water from a stream to a lower level
5. a dense growth of trees and underbrush covering a large area
6. a large body of water that flows overland in a long channel

bridge
forest
highway
island
lake
marina
mountain
railway
river
waterfall

Answer Key

Page 1
Across
3. horse
4. cow
5. pigs
7. goat
9. rabbit

Down
1. sheep
2. chicken
6. goose
8. turkey

Page 2
Across
4. light
5. file
7. pound
8. ball

Down
1. rattle
2. plant
3. kind
6. hand
7. play

Page 3
Across
1. pickup
2. tank
4. van
5. dump
7. concrete

Down
1. platform
3. garbage
6. panel van

Pages 4–5
Across
1. Mouse
4. Jack and Jill
6. Old Woman
7. Peter
8. Cow
10. Little Bo Peep
11. Mary

Down
2. Spider
3. Humpty Dumpty
4. Jack
5. London
9. Three

Page 6
Across
5. umbrella
6. postcard
9. holiday
10. pool
11. car
12. aeroplane
14. tourist
15. suitcase

Down
1. kennel
2. souvenir
3. boat
4. map
7. camping
8. vacation
13. hotel
14. train

Page 7
Across
2. spinnerets
6. poison
8. insect
9. bones

Down
1. silk
3. eight
4. two
5. food
7. webs

Page 8
Across
1. bee
4. horse fly
6. termite
7. mayfly
8. ant
9. dragonfly

Down
1. butterfly
2. mosquito
3. firefly
5. ladybug

Page 9
Across
1. buzz
3. jingle
4. pop
6. crash
8. meow

Down
1. beep
2. hiss
5. peep
6. click
7. tweet

Page 10
Across
1. roots
3. wood
5. evergreen
7. food
8. botanists
9. soil and water

Down
2. seed
4. deciduous
6. grow

Page 11
Across
2. lungs
5. temperature
7. dinosaur
8. land

Down
1. plates
3. backbone
4. reptiles
6. shell

Page 12
Across
4. whisper
5. scream
7. joke
8. chat

Down
1. discuss
2. speak
3. brag
6. report

Page 13
Across
3. kelp forests
6. sea horse
8. roots
9. coral reefs

Down
1. waves
2. rockfish
4. tidal pools
5. polyps
7. tides

Page 14
Across
5. carbohydrates
6. milk
7. starches
8. fat
9. salt
10. pasta

Down
1. sugar
2. fruits
3. meat
4. vegetables

Page 15
Across
3. honeycomb
6. flowers
8. insects

Down
1. drones
2. worker
3. honey
4. hives
5. queen's
7. sting

Pages 16–17
Across
1. giraffe
5. bat
6. elk
7. horse
9. cat
10. zebra
11. wolf
13. hippo

Down
1. goat
2. rabbit
3. elephant
4. whale
8. raccoon
9. cheetah
12. fox

Page 18
Across
1. cabin
4. apartment
7. houseboat
8. roof
10. igloo

Down
1. cottage
2. walls
3. castle
5. teepee
6. door
9. floor

Page 19
Across
2. rain forests
4. salt water
8. ocean
10. wetland

Down
1. grasslands
3. desert
5. tundra
6. forest
7. ponds
9. swamps

Pages 20–21
Across
2. elephants
5. acrobats
8. trapeze
9. horses
10. jugglers
11. roustabouts
13. Big Top

Down
1. band
3. parade
4. rings
6. costumes
7. clowns
8. tigers
12. tricks

Page 22
Across
3. table tennis
5. softball
6. bowling
9. football

Down
1. volleyball
2. basketball
3. tennis
4. squash
6. baseball
7. golf
8. soccer

Page 23
Across
3. fat
5. polar bear
7. skin
9. rubbery
10. front

Down
1. walrus
2. fur
4. hoofs
6. hibernate
8. zero

Page 24
Across
2. Go
3. Trivial Pursuit
4. Cluedo
5. Chess
7. Snakes & Ladders

Down
1. Monopoly
4. Checkers
6. Scrabble

Page 25
Across
1. snowboarding
3. soccer
5. tennis
7. baseball
9. hockey
10. golf

Down
1. skateboarding
2. basketball
4. bowling
6. football
8. squash

Page 26
Across
3. avalanche
5. tornado
7. earthquake
8. hurricane

Down
1. cyclones
2. blizzard
4. flood
5. tsunami
6. typhoons

Page 27
Across
2. salt
3. steer
5. mammals
7. blowhole
8. seals

Down
1. water
3. surface
4. walrus
6. blue

Pages 28–29
Across
3. Gutenberg
5. Lister
6. Edison
7. Kellogg

Down
1. Wright
2. Benz and Daimler
3. Graham Bell
4. Franklin

Page 30
Across
4. light
5. file
7. pound
8. ball

Down
1. rattle
2. plant
3. kind
6. hand
7. play

Page 31
Across

A. 22	B. 105		
C. 29	D. 17		
E. 12	F. 12		
G. 105	H. 28		
I. 85	J. 16		

Down

A. 296	B. 105
C. 222	D. 15
E. 12	F. 18
G. 15	H. 236
I. 85	

Page 32
Across
4. oil
5. hummingbirds
8. toes

Down
1. frog
2. down
3. straight
6. molt
7. cones

Page 33
Across
5. carbohydrates
6. milk
7. starches
8. fat
9. salt
10. pasta

Down
1. sugar
2. fruits
3. meat
4. vegetables

Answer Key

Page 34

Across
1. players
7. racket
9. love
10. doubles
11. set
12. net

Down
1. point
2. ace
3. singles
4. deuce
5. service
6. ball
8. court

Page 35

Across
b. quotient
d. fraction
g. denominator
h. divisor
i. product
j. sets
k. factors

Down
a. sum
c. numerator
e. remainder
f. difference
g. dividend

Pages 36–37

Across
2. Greyhound
6. Retriever
7. Setter
8. Afghan
10. Boxer
11. Dalmation

Down
1. Husky
2. Great Dane
3. Dachshund
4. Pointer
5. Beagle
9. Poodle

Pages 38–39

Across
1. bus
2. truck
3. motorcycle
4. train

Down
1. bicycle
2. tram
5. taxi
6. car

Page 40

Across
1. passengers
3. control tower
6. tickets
7. hangars
8. gate
10. baggage

Down
1. pilot
2. security guards
4. runways
5. terminal
9. fuel

Page 41

Across
5. square
6. rectangle
7. cone
8. cylinder

Down
1. circle
2. sphere
3. triangle
4. cube

Page 42

Across
1. mosquito
3. cockroach
5. vampire
6. fleas
9. gypsy moth

Down
2. scorpion
4. housefly
7. termites
8. rat

Page 43

Across
1. temperature
3. weather
7. precipitation
8. condensation

Down
2. evaporation
4. air pressure
5. water
6. wind

Page 44

Across
1. grow
2. mammals
4. capybaras
5. diseases
6. rodents
8. herbivorous

Down
1. gnawing
2. mice
3. scientists
7. fur

Page 45

Across
2. pitcher
6. diamond
7. bat
8. five
9. umpire
11. base
12. outfield
13. glove

Down
1. strike
3. home
4. run
5. catcher
8. fly ball
10. inning
12. outs

Page 46

Across
2. carnivore
4. water cycle
6. habitat
7. ecology
8. herbivore
9. omnivores
10. botany

Down
1. parasite
3. meteorology
5. oxygen

Page 47

Across
1. eyes
2. muscles
4. heart
5. lungs
7. brain

Down
1. ears
3. skeleton
6. skin
7. blood

Pages 48–49

Across
2. printing press
3. television
4. satellite
5. computer
6. map
7. wheel
8. camera
9. aeroplane

Down
1. microscope
2. plough
3. telephone
5. clock

Page 50

Across
1. sunspots
5. galaxy
6. life
7. light & heat
10. yellow dwarf

Down
1. solar flares
2. star
3. gas
4. Milky Way
8. energy
9. core

Page 51

Across
2. pronouns
5. nouns
6. interjections
7. adverbs

Down
1. conjunctions
2. prepositions
3. adjectives
4. verbs

Page 52

Across
5. hurricane
6. funnel
8. cyclone
9. tornado
10. blizzard

Down
1. open
2. thunder
3. rain
4. cumulonimbus
7. cold

Page 53

Across
3. food
4. leaves
5. roots
7. life
8. water
10. sunlight
11. clothes
12. seeds

Down
1. photosynthesis
2. medicines
4. litter
6. shelter
9. air

Page 54

Across
1. cinematographer
2. screenwriter
3. producer
5. documentaries
8. art director
9. Oscar

Down
1. costume designer
4. director
6. animation
7. actors

Page 55

Across
4. curved
6. parallelogram
8. edge
9. sphere
11. trapezoid
12. line
13. angle

Down
1. symmetry
2. perimeter
3. hexagon
5. congruent
7. area
9. solid
10. face

Pages 56–57

Across
2. Mars
3. Moon
4. Uranus
6. Saturn
8. Jupiter
9. Pluto
10. Earth

Down
1. Venus
2. Mercury
5. Sun
7. Neptune

Page 58

Across
1. glaciers
4. high-altitude
5. Wyoming
7. magma
9. Congress

Down
2. Louisiana Purchase
3. petrified
6. geyser
8. rocks

Page 59

Across
1. Amazon
3. petroleum
5. Brazil
6. Andes
8. Colombia

Down
1. Angel Falls
2. Pampa
4. rain
7. Ecuador

Page 60

Across
1. stadium
3. school
4. castle
7. hospital

Down
1. skyscraper
2. museum
5. hotel
6. house

Page 61

Across
3. minerals
4. diamond
6. microscope
8. sedimentary

Down
1. igneous
2. hardness
3. metamorphic
5. fossils
7. magma

Page 62

Across
2. highway
7. mountain
8. bridge
9. marina
10. railroad

Down
1. lake
3. island
4. waterfall
5. forest
6. river